TREADWINDS

TREADWINDS

poems and

intermedia

texts

Walter K. Lew

Wesleyan University Press
Middletown, Connecticut

Published by Wesleyan University Press,

Middletown, CT 06459

Copyright © 2002 by Walter K. Lew

ISBN 0-8195-6509-1 cloth

ISBN 0-8195-6510-5 paper

Printed in the United States of America

Design and composition by

B. Williams & Associates, Durham, NC

5   4   3   2   1

CiP data appear at the end of the book.

For the many scattered leaves of the 李 and 柳 trees
Both here and afar

Beneath the bleeding hands we feel
The sharp compassion of the healer's art

Contents

Treadwinds

天文學

Early on we learned
That when we couldn't see the face
It was still there
Later, we covered that
Wound up with speech. But words also
Disappeared, could not
Repeat forever
And more and more
Things would not return to us
When we said them. Here, they said
Learn this.
        A song, a story
And though things are no longer near

You will see how they have changed.

    •

À la fin tu es las des rêves nouvelles

Though we can't know in the end if it is *all* a spell

Who would to be asked?

The beginning of questions we can hardly face

Perhaps it's a dream I had when five

And remembered as real when fifteen, permanent
Blur and diffraction   [Diffraction in my depths
In my depths.

It doesn't matter: there are
Equations, they tell us

Facts about the light its
Aberration and flawing

We make our laws up out of

fear and tenacity

and find in them

faits about the light, its

aberration and flawing

Whenever a planet

Wheels all hell-like
Grinding in the wrong

[Azimuth or angle of
Right-ascension: coordinates

Deep in the lake of the heart

Long ago, there was a youth who got a bad palm reading. Afterwards, he worked hard at trying to cut good lines into his palms.

— Kim Sŭng-ok

I went in white pants
To the ancestral mounds.
When I fell into a paddy
My brain seeped.

Soft-eyed oxen raised me
Up to a thatched roof to dry.
At dusk, the farmer's wife fed me
In strips to her children.

That evening, down at the makkoli house
The farmer stood up in the middle of a song,
Bet a hill and three daughters
That no one could guess

What had been dug up in his fields that day.

LEAVING SEOUL: 1953

We have to bury the urns,
Mother and I. We tried to leave them in a back room,
Decoyed by a gas lamp, and run out

But they landed behind us here, at the front gate.
It is 6th hour, early winter, black cold:
Only, on the other side of the rice-paper doors

The yellow ondol stone-heated floors
Are still warm. I look out to the blue
Lanterns along the runway, the bright airplane.

Off the back step, Mother, disorganized
As usual, has devised a clumsy rope and shovel
To bury the urns. I wonder out loud

How she ever became a doctor.
Get out, she says. *Go to your father: he too*
Does not realize what is happening. You see,

Father is waiting at the airfield in a discarded U.S. Army
Overcoat. He has lost his hat, lost
His father, and is smoking Lucky's like crazy....

We grab through the tall weeds and wind
That begin to shoot under us like river ice.
It is snowing. We are crying, from the cold

Or what? It is only decades
Later that, tapping the glowing jars,
I find they contain all that has made
The father have dominion over hers.

MOUND 1: SILENT FOR TWENTY-FIVE YEARS, THE FATHER OF MY MOTHER ADVISES ME

I

Careless
but not fearless

You spin out for the great cities:
hang-outs, libraries
heavy-boned churches
you never knew the magic of

Subway troubadours
taxicab Orphées
Dump you wind-stroked in the larynx
of alley after alley, contemplating

Light petaling through fire escapes
like your own seasons, like the one
long season you hesitate
to dig up and divine: Ours, and not of those

Leaping by in the snow-lit mouth
behind you, beyond the dumpster
To swirl down numbered Aves
with the cars and commerce

Everything with its colors
on, everything marked to leave your
Own 詩 heart, own mouth magic
SHI   gabbing to a brick

•

As you sprint away from me
your hair lengthens,
bounds, like the billowing squid-
dyed flame of ocean

I once saw unfurl across
a kabuki stage when I was
a foreign student of law
at a Tokyo university.

Tied to my bones
your hair is taut,
twists in the riven
spewing hole of mud

Above me, and as the sky and moon
run right to the edge
of the hills around
my grave, and you chase

The melon light down
the far faces,
your scalp's sinews
rear and gasp: Resound

before they snap, yanked
snarling through the dust
collapsing behind you: tendon, weeds,
lizard, pod snagged

In the lash at the end
Of each resinous strand.
Here, in the mound
I hold on to this end.

II

Come up the dust road,
Across the reservoir, along
The muddy ridges of the toad-sung
Paddies, past the farmer-gravekeeper's house.

Tell his children rinsing
Melons at the pump, you'll stop in later;
Even if he greets you, do not pause
For makkoli or chatter.

At the burial slope's gate
The road ends like an uplifted tongue.
With your touch read
The stele there, and climb up

And bow down three times before each living
Nourishing, wild-haired mound,
Before each of the generations:
And know clearly, sonja

Our reply
By the song of the crickets there.

•

The taste of rough grass
And clay still curling in my mouth,
I took the form of a snake
Pierced your burrow, and took at last
My place at the table of the dead.

There, the brass-lidded bowls filled with
Uncooked rice and the silver bowls
Of cold broth caked over with beef fat
Like a skating pond, bone ends
Jutting up around

Frozen, crimson marrow,
Had been waiting for years to release
Their light in me.
Through the open back passage

I saw that even the tall crocks
Of soy, of thick, sweet pepper paste
Had also been waiting, shoulder-deep
In the cold earth pit.

As I ate they embraced my tongue, teeth, gullet,
In me were threshed and germinated.

I finished the meal alone, Grandfather,
Wept against the blood-warmed earth
And sung the lullaby Father would dissolve
    my nightmares with . . .

                                        Cha-jháng, cha-jháng

I dust off the photographs
Cinder the incense
Arrange the rice cakes
And gold-flecked root

I dressed you in the white ramie and cotton,
Covered you with brocaded quilts,
And felt and heard those things
I cannot speak of yet.

Cha-jháng . . .

And you said,
        "Now go home, sonja,
                            Kyu-sŭng-ah!
With the dark scroll I have just
Unrolled for you—for you alone

To peruse and be puzzled by
The rest of your days. Sing of us dead,
We are alive. Yes, return
Now Poet 诗

人

SHI-IN
To the text you have just
Begun to write."

量－無－故－如－恒－相　佛　大－不－亦－形－本－刹

無　含－十－方－刹　本　國　切－一－切－法－中－一

數　包　塵－切－一　刹　容　解　量－無－一－於－解　刹

曠　塵　中　曠－大－諸　十　中　法　佛－士－滿－十－方

大　一　皆　增－塵－一　法　一　則　一－法－量－無－是

劫　累　如－是－不－令　界　者　是－一－法－一－法－則

智　重－了－知－界－世　諸　而　智－體－槃－涅－提－菩　是

者－求－方－十－則－一　一　念　生－死－涅－槃－非－異－處　則

成－求　方　知　詣　一　槃　難－甚－而－近－提　煩　處

佛－不－知－身　遍　念　涅　見－身－心－本　菩　惱　佳

佛－成－舊－心　促　未　則　滅－生－無－來　談　菩　無

往　亦－不－縮　成　曾　死　一　親－而－無－人　提　滅

昔　劫－長－遠　長　演　生　切　槃－涅－二－無－體　無

精－進－捨－生－死－不－知　諸－法－亦－如－是－無－生

DOWN FROM THE MONASTERY

Priest Baba jabs
quickly through a spill of photographs
and finds a tiny sepia tint

of five Korean schoolgirls in hanbok
Curved together on a wild hill,
sky-drunk as they gaze off

Over the camera,
Part of the Japanese empire.
Some hold onto stalks
Of pampas grass, the wind is that strong
And certain clouds are about to
Slide away forever.
Baba slaps his feet and sighs:
"That mood will never return.
Too bad you didn't live then
You could have fallen in love with a country girl
When you were 14 or 15 and
Written a beautiful sad story."
He points at the most dewy-faced girl:
"Maybe she was never that pretty again!" I tell him,
That's my mother! I knew that, he laughs, then shuts up
        to not
Parch their gazes.
For a moment I imagine
He is about to sing another bar song,
But he doesn't. He makes me promise
I'll read the sutras

Then goes down the hall to get me cold water
Because "guys" my age always eat so fast
They forget to drink with their food.

Baba, why did you laugh so hard?
You can't even remember your mother.

When you were a boy chanting
Kwanseŭm posal, Kwanseŭm posal
All dawn in the mountain temple,
You kept saying *inside*
Omŏni ŏdi, Omŏni ŏdi—Where's
my mommy Where's my mommy
When you beat all the orphan taunters
With your dragon drawings
And returned with the valley school's prize,
A bad monk tore them up and said, "Can you make
Rice with this? Will it
Bring your mommy back?"
                              Bless, you said
The old ill priest who rose from his cell,
Pieced the paper back together,
Blew dirt off the gleaming dragon eyes,
And kept winking as he praised them.
Unwrapping candy, he made you promise to continue
Even if he leaves soon.

Baba, let's wander together—
It's true we still have pictures

But have lost our souls. Let us lose
Our loss together
And feed at last

The children cold inside us.

Kwanseŭm posal, Kwanseŭm posal

All dawn in the mountain temple

aracter for thing, mulgon]

 There

[heavily struck-through lines, illegible]
...an ideal thing...
...And yet imperfections...one
...exaggerate and pretend...

aracter for aboji]

 father

bring you from the shades, I had
hhad

aracter for aboji]

father

brangeyonoofrahoshé shades I had

father

bring you from the shades I had
aracter for aboji]

Th
 father

bring you from the sh

H SEEMED A SORT OF DELIBERATE OR CONTRIVED SELF-DISADVANTAGING

anater for aboji]

father

ring you from the shades, I had to stubbornly wander in those regions you so w

ring you from the shades, I had

ring you from the shades, I had to deliberately wander in regions
so willfully stumbled out of.

ring you from the shades, I had to stubbornly wander, like a
 in the regions you so willfully stumbled out of. You must have
ered: Why return to the realms of pain? That was never an issue
e, though others did disparage what seemed to be my foolishness,

Father,
Under a thin moon
They'll spit out your only son's names:
Disobedient, Failure, No Wife

And even that will not hurt you:
All you wanted for him was
Safe,
      Plenty of Cash,
            No Death

But it's your past too
I am searching for. Its summer, its
Winter. Father, I'm going

Out to talk with the crewcut boy
Who sat at the sunny south window
    and read
Boy's Life and Goethe, *Segye Munhak*

In characters that shaded like paulownia leaves
Thoughts of striped melons cooling in the well
While the rice blew in the east fields.

I'm sneaking round to the front porch
And placing my hands on the father
You would lose in '50
In Seoul
Just like that
Though you bicycled for days north and south and
Back again, calling his name
While the tank volley and mortar came down.
Yes! He is
Back from the job in Manchuria he took
To pay your tuition at proud KS:

He kneels in the doorway
Lights a long pipe, smiles as he watches you
Trim a fresh kite—almost
Breathing the real world

I am putting my hand on his shoulder, Father
And I am dragging him back,
I am dragging every strand and wisp of his
Unmarkered, unworshiped soul back

And Father,
Most wondrous thing

Kŭrŏnde, Appa!

He is asking me to do this.

During their heyday in the 1920s and 1930s, Korean pyŏnsa, or "movietellers," provided live narration for silent and untranslated films. Seated between the audience and projection screen, the pyŏnsa alternated between third-person narrative, impersonations of each character in the film, commentary (often disguised criticism of Japanese colonial rule), and the making of sound effects, such as storm winds and the clopping of horses' hooves.

I left Seoul in the winter of 1935,
When the biggest show in town
Was Greta Garbo in Queen Christina.

Just a year before, it would have been me
And not some faceless, dubbed-in English major

Who made Garbo speak in Korean,
For I was still the reigning Pyŏnsa
In the grand Myŏngdong movie houses.

The talkies came in
And I fell silent. . . .
                    In Tokyo, the first release bombed
Was greeted with yells
To shut the sound off and get

A "benshi" up there—And one
Movietellers federation
Unwired the new expensive systems,
                                got soused & danced
When the first sound films flopped.
                            (That was before the Right Wing
    rose and crushed the Left,
    both there and here.)

    But soon people liked
    A void between

    Themselves and the screen,
    Where I used to sit

And say what they saw—sound effects too!
안되었어요!

•

That *Christina* was playing
was especially irritating:
Garbo had been my favorite.
I even took delight in her big feet and bent shins.
Moreover, it had been exactly on my
20th birthday that the chubby
Teen-aged Stockholm model
(Not embittered yet by Hollywood mogul
    Louis B. Mayer),
Changed her last name from Gustafsson to Garbo—
"I want," said her agent Stiller, "a name that's . . .

International, that means the same and says
Who she is in Paris as clearly as in
    Budapest and New York."
A name that *did* eventually glimmer
Imperial and alone

On every movie hall marquee
In the modernized world.

    And it was I who was almost fired
    For refusing to let our theater degrade her
    With a tasteless advertising kit
    From MGM via Tokyo:

Bland line drawings of her in different poses & costumes that could be
blown up for billboards, newspapers, shadow-boxes, trolley cards, side-
walk stencils, circus flyers, advance lobby placards, and street signs &
arrows:
    GARBO rumbas the Chicachoca!
    GARBO has a twin! And she's double-trouble for Melvyn Douglas!
    GARBO introduces the Foolscap! A hat destined to be as
        revolutionary as her famous Pillbox!
    GARBO swims! Like a Mer—mai——id. . . .

Our P.R. man—a Mr. Kim who, anticipating Japanese trade, had
eagerly changed his name to Kanemoto before the law required it,
always pushed to do any stunt that the studios suggested. I said: Just
put her name in the paper next to mine—that will make her sell.
And, of course, she did.

But she also sold herself to sound,
Betraying me.
       Sure, I read about
Her fear of talkies, how
Uncertain she was of her English, and that
She was so nervous about her sound test
That she stayed up the whole night before
Chatting with her confidant, William Sorenson
(whom I deeply envied).
       Still, it rekindled her career
While killing mine.
       So what? you say, but look—
Talk all you want about
Great stars and directors:
In Seoul it was the best pyŏnsa
That people lined up for!

       I began before leaving technical school,
Telling the Max Fleischer cartoons and Chūshingura they showed
Saturday afternoons on the top floor
Of the Hwashin department store.
Then came offers from
Big cinemas downtown . . .
       I could not resist: Ciao!
I said to my chemistry comrades
And splurged at Mitsukoshi's
On a herring-bone oba
And some Roman pomade.

       The first days, I must admit,
I barely managed:
I sometimes didn't know the movies any better

Than the audience did.
Then a friend told me it didn't matter. In fact,
There was a benshi in Osaka
Who never cared what happened in foreign films:
He would simply call the hero "Jyani-sama,"
The girl he saved or died on "Mari-sama,"
All the bad guys "Raja," and rattled off his own naniwabushi
Souped up with
Packards, gats, Indians who ran into cavalry charges,
And various exotic scenes—speakeasies, for example, or
Ballrooms and wagon trains.

But the talkies came in and we fell silent,

>   The people soon liking a void between
>   Themselves and the screen,

>   Where we used to sit
>   And say what they saw—Sound effects, too!
>   Andweŏssŏ-yo. . . .

And so I became, more and more, a mere
Spectator:

Angry at scenes that weren't well lip-synched
Or the tinny lushness of orchestral
[Audiotape: "Home on the Range" from Gary Cooper film The Cowboy and
the Lady]
backgrounds.

[Movieteller bows his head in dejection and turns off reading lamp.]

End of scene 2

Children shone in the front gate and put their hands together in the demon pavilion.

Then they went up red-dusted steps toward the granite stupa, where they didn't hesitate to bow with their mothers.

Thick white candles with reverse swastikas and rows of images on the ascending plinths of stone.

I crouched under the temple, in the cool shadow, by the outdoor Nestlé's coffee dispenser—and was aroused when two women strode by in russet hanbok

"Color of the dharma's robes," said monk Sŏgu suddenly beside me.

I followed him down the hill and sat on a log. There was a small lake and I was calm enough at last to listen to my new uncle conduct the neighborhood's Bodhisattva orchestra, seated on folding chairs in the mud beside it.

신발을벗어버린발이虛天에서失足한다.

　　　　　　　　　　　　　　　　　　一李箱

BRINE

I

My woman's blood
Is of dark and salt.
She has a clay, red mouth

Which I mouth, but it will not
Sing or seal.

II

When I eat her blood
I return down a smooth dune
From the hills, and enter

A raspberry path: my mouth and fingers
stained ripe.

III

Grass, mist and sand
My woman's blood
Is of loam and rain.

With sleek wings she combs
My bloated sides

Whispers,
And the ear is a conch

Our heads shake
And hair is a grove,

The baywind luffing
Black shocks of
Reed and laver.

IV

Morning blooms on the stained linen.
Sea mist on her hairs
Curls round my fingers

       On that short, fine lawn
       Wet crystals bead. In her
       Thick wound, rubies smear
       Like fish eggs.

V

When she is not here all week
I walk around this same town
And all the storefronts seem hushed
And flimsy, as if my eyes, salt-crystaled
Could only dwell in her
Dense light. Dark city!

       Four days I wore her deep ink
       Down my waist and
       Along my thighs, like a jeweled
       Girdle.

VI

I wait at the station
My mouth, organs
Like a flock of mussels, shut up
To sun
And hands

Until their green wave revives.

DRIVING BACK FROM THE ROSY-FINGERED BERKSHIRES

I

White, and low on the left
Holyoke, some town
Stunned with mist.

On the right, black crags
Of anthracite, young birch leaning out
Like village kids.

I am well rested. The musk
Of the Macintosh Red my girlfriend gave me
Tinctures the car
With the sunrise.

II

At Hartford,
A station wagon veers away at Exit 4—
Its family, soiled as a dishrag
Smearing its face in the window.

On a gully turn, I near a long
Trailer-load of lumber;
If I listen close enough above
The wash of tires, I can almost hear
The screaming of squirrels,
Or is it the sounds
Of a new house?

III

Dusk, at New Haven I pass one by one
Squat yellow jitneys
Carrying schoolchildren, steered by beautiful
Graying women. One is wearing
A necklace of beads as large and hard

As their orange eyes
Of sunset that I watch in the mirror
As they fall behind, staring into the horizon
Like the faces of their trucks, the chatter behind them
Invisible.

IV

Four more hours
I will be back in Baltimore.
My mother leaves work early
To prepare the thick
Kalbi and dumpling soup
She promised last night by phone.
"If you could bring the right girl home. . . ."

And my father
Flies round the hospital
Tending his patients,
Still thinking bitterly of how I
Just walked away from med school.

I search and search my tiny heart
And am astonished to find
No pain, no
Anger at all. My car

Eats the lines on the highway
Like spears of old light,
And lays down darkness behind it.

I lift my hand from the dial and watch the sun move
    to you in the West. I am sitting at the tall
South window and can see the chorus of four downtown
    towers and the small church domes
In front of them. I open the chipped
    shutters and watch dark streams
Of silhouetted heat flow toward me over this
    half-filled sheet and my wrists, as the sun breaks
A thick cloud gut and inverts the whole scene
    Before me!—negative roofs and building
        flanks now
    Sopped with its flame. The sun ⴃ
                facing me now
From the clip of my pen throws quick trihedrons
    like water dazzle, like the wings of mayflies
About the room. Now I rise, roam after these
    flashes of your voice
My wanded left hand and ring finger making
    as I chase, light dance on further and further surfaces like
The telephone, bright breakfast
    Scraps or the orchestral blazing door before me,
    Sinking as it opens
                into your sea.

(for SL)

JUST-NO TALE

A boy and girl play on the lawn.
That's where it all begins! When I was five

My mother sent me to spend a day
With an Austrian gynecologist's pretty daughter

I had a crush on—Or was it the mother I was feverish for?
I loved her black stockings and the week before

She had laughed to see me in a corner of her office
Squatting lower and lower into my bursting gut

To gaze at the back of her knees whenever her
White lab coat lifted around them. She clucked

And a sprig of reddish blond hair fingering her brow
She asked if I liked her new nylons, and smiled like

Mercy, mercy as she hiked her frock and tweed skirt up
One gleaming thigh till I rose sharply

Back in embarrassed fainting glee, reached out
For the cold stirrups of the examining table.

My mother may have known about this
When she took me to play with Suzy. It was O.K.—

She had good toys. But late in the afternoon
After I taught her how to wear a six-shooter and cavalry scarf

And we skirmished each other for a while,
I called time-out and motioned her to the middle of the yard

As if I had some great secret to tell her
Forbidden by the grown-up world. Oh, how that girl

Trusted me, her Danube eyes! She was only
Inches away and I kept pulling her in

With my whispers, ducked head and flagging hands.
Then I pushed her, threw her back hard as I could, the tin pistol

Flew back and cut her mouth and I walked off to seethe
In the fenced corner. She cried the rest of the day and Dr. Fromm

Made me sit on the living room couch, without snacks
Or picture books until my mother picked me up.

I didn't feel sorry, I hated Suzy's howling and wanted
To shout like a madman until everything stopped. When I left

The mother and daughter were nice enough to wave goodbye
From behind a screen door, and their spaniel barked on the flagstone
    walk.

I've been smiling about this all day, my love
As we push each other away.

THE STARS AND STRIPES

I

Saturday night: in beat-up cars, the art school
Gay begin to cruise. Or maybe
They're lowlifes from downtown and Johnston
Thinking I'm from the School of Design.
(I attend the university even further up the Hill.)
One load screams out, "Needa ride?
Wanna slide?" Two blocks down, a thin
Blond pulls up, expired tags from Illinois:
"Looks like yours should fit the bill—
Do join me, pretty boy."

II

The quickness
Of my refusal
Startles me
Now. I wrap myself
In blankets,
Say and taste
The names of old
Flames. On the cold
Dark mattress,
I hug my loneliness
And know it is
Common. It lies beside me
Now like stone,
Now like a stranger, sympathetically
Known.

III

Way past two,
A Chevy waits under
The flushed hands of her
Slumped-over driver. The sweet gas fume

Wells up trees at the sash I left open
For the breeze waved through

With the wet moon and incense
Of maple leaf rotting. Far down
In the pit of Providence
As I blur into sleep, I perceive

The silent flag, arc-lit against
The new conglomerate's fifty-two floors,
How it sags, then lashes out as before
Pinned to its pole
Like a huge flame:
Blood-striped, blue and
Distant all the same.

In 1937, the court, citing historical circumstances and
the victim's acquiescence, acquitted Sada of blame in her
employer's death and dismemberment.

I

Shya, sha the summer rain
Outside. Even the barber's blade
Wilts for a moment, like a faraway tide
Waves flashing in front of
The customer's eye.

The name of the customer is Kichizo,
Geisha-house owner.
He has so far evaded

Conscription.

II

December's shigure, shigu—
In a paper rain cape,
he hops from the tin
barbershop, its shiny hiragana sign
looping broken
                        into the sky
like a half-written
wreck. He slogs left, then
Left again through deep mud
on geta. Where is
pure winter light, "hawk
majestic on a snowy pine branch"?

Wound in steam,
he stops at a cart for a bowl of noodles.
He smokes half a cigarette, then tamps it out.

He cuts the ash end off and wraps
the rest up for his lover, strumming
a shamisen at the inn.

III

As he drifts back,
he dances the stupid
song she is singing.

He walks in the shadow of rusted eaves
as the bayoneted river
of recruits bends toward him,
up the main road

out of town. On either side,
a deep bank
of quiet women wave them on,

White and scarlet
flags, scarves gushing like camellia
from their wrists. They wave and wave:
How unbearable the female silence!
And all the soldiers say
is jya, jya.
                    He
Doesn't mock or stare
But takes the back way sure
Of the blood between his thighs:
After he climbs back into his room
And slides shut the shōji door,
He helps his lover bend it back upon him
Until the awed and swordless casualty sighs.

タンビというおんなが
とっても... なんと
いいますか？

なんというかどうかわからない。

タンビが
　　　　BAMBIじゃ
　　　　　　ありませんよ!!!

　ほんとう。

タンビのほんみょうがひみつですね。それははずかしいだからおしえて
くれなかったんです。ぼくもしりたくはありませんでした。

わたくしもしりたくない。

鏡 一

Tambi to you: No honor got
outta my non-toy
Miss Cigar.

Non-toy: caddy,
　　　　　　　川
car at nine . . .

Tambi's got,
　　　　Bambi not
A rhyme & sense zombie arm scent, yo!

"Hon" to

Tambi—No hon's more
Guy mit pseudo-knee. Beau cd mo . . . share it, ax you, "Wire my
Sens, d'Shitta?"

Sore wa hazukashii kara osiete kurenakatta to iun

What a cushy mo. Shirr it—*Aigyu!* nigh.

　　　　　　　　　　　　　　　　　　　　鏡二

AN APARTMENT IN THE CITY

Her new flat
West Village
"Good part of the country"
What I always

Wanted: 1200, A/C
high walls.
                         Stockings of her apt. mate—
Would like you,
      likes Korean food.
"Fucks like a bunny." (Ray)
     Ray! "Kicked me in the disco,
              didn't say a thing, then
              she hit me again
              in front of the Coke machine.
     Shit . . . what you do then?
              Didn't do a thing. Bitch
              went up to the room. Hey,
              Where else could she go?"

Goes to the couch
To turn A/C on—jesus, her hair, shoulders, and
back of knee. Miles' E.S.P.
on a good Sansui. "Iris." Iris
Herbie's perfect chords—   Herbie
                          Don't play like that
                          Anymore!
Doesn't matter. For her
It's a mood. 1200!

What I made the last two months, sometimes hustling
A kid, me.
But she
Honest
Money,

Father a good doctor.
Little sparkplug,
Jumped up and crooned
With B.B. "The Thrill is gone!" who
Teased him with Lucille
And told him sit the hell down.
"Good doctor."
Up at Sinai,
Jew help a Jew.
Buys "the poor kid's paintings" In spare time,
Keeps up on Tel Aviv poets
Unlike Mr. Kim, who thinks literature went out with
Yangban and Confucius.   Doesn't know his characters
                    but crazy about Jeejush
                    Reads Yohan again & again
                    While running a fruit stand
                    with wife and kids up on
                    Amsterdam. 80 hrs/wk 6 years. Just bought
                    a Cape Cod in Mt. Vernon.
                    Son's an accountant, daughter plays
                    the violin: Dartmouth, Juilliard.
                    Wife got shot

                    tending the shop at 3 in the morning.
                    Why the fuck was she alone?
                    That's not the point.
                    Kkamdung-i did it.
                    That's not the point. Then,

                    Stupid cousin blew away
                    Nigger cunt next Sunday.
                    Dancer. Friend cries out
                    She just went in for a box of tampons, man!
                    Koreans crazy
                    Run half of Harlem.
                    Walk around the warehouses
                    like wolves. Stink. Blood
                    in their eyes. Chinks and Niggers
                    (Aint *Chinese*, you asshole!)
                    Killing each other over

What? Of course don't have no time for your
stupid lit'chwer. Why can't you
speak Korean? Go
to med school. . . .

She broils a few big sea scallops
With lemon up for me.
Real coffee-table books on a coffee table.
Rug you wouldn't mind getting buried in.
We go out to the balcony: "There,

And there!" she laughs
Pointing at windows
Where people are making love or taking their clothes off.
But I look at the pianos
Pianos. I say, *Look, I can't pretend*
anymore . . . and place my hands like octaves
    into
  The humid breeze.
                  The record stops
  And "Mood"'s
  Last perfect chord goes out
  Like a sigh, a star, like a burning prayer
  Over the cooling, scarred rooftops.

1977

All things you can C-sharp.

—Charles Mingus

TWO HANDFULS OF WAKA FOR THELONIOUS SPHERE MONK
(d. Feb. 1982)

When Monk laid it down
Each note would blur a moment and
Pass on: pure, midnight.

Cut into time like ruby:
In the hard, celestial chord.

    •

Passed on pure, midnight:
Now they tune the stars like sharps,
Jar the dark alive

And the cold space carves his song
Till it pierces the other world

    •

Jars the dark. Alive?
A priest did say, "He is
Received into bliss

      Eternal—jamming with God's best
      in that Great hymn of Praise. . . ."

True, he is freed from
Misery of this or that.
But also things like

      Green Chimneys, Off Minors, and
      Billie Holiday in red

Can no more wander
In his stride, slide and wangle . . .
Close to the end of

      the world anyway: What difference a
      Misterioso or Epistrophy?

    •

Still, when in the quartz
Chapel, strong Randy Weston
Raised Monk's song, hundreds

    In their midtown scramble paused,
    Seraphing the high windows

Galleries, aisles,
And crowded the pulpit, budged
The altar. It was

    Not you and yet your time in
    Randy's hands did illumine each

Mind. We knew your song
Not heaven, was the great sphere
And that it was for us

    to play it at our best—
    Received now into Thelonious,

I Mean You, into
Humph and Introspection: their key
Eternal bliss

    Though it is only now,
    Near the end of the world

    •

That we might pass on
What he taught us to hear: the silent
Trembling inside

    Each beat; the distance between
    The Raised 1 and Flat 2:

Ourselves and Ourselves.
As Monk laid it down and
Passed on: pure, round

    Midnight

PASSING UNDER THE MOUNTAIN

for R, poet and pianist of the Arcanum

Strychnine, you whispered
And gazed as if it were chipped
From a crystalline sphere of angels.

One more eccentric phase?
But if Orpheus plucks beyond
Drawing singers to a rest, a final
Quaver in resonant wells,
And if the young (as was told) ply
A straighter route of ascension. . . .

You held in your lungs like quartz;
A stripe of blood
Dried up on your vocal cords.

•

You broke to leave
The arterial word,
To blunt the heave
Of jazz, to cut away
The flesh that quakes
Above a poem, like dying Trane
Around his horn,
The eyeless fingers
Still fleet
Along the keys.

In the twilight, all the pianos
Tensed for a moment,
Gleaming like marble sluices.

•

Hatred of the mortal's tongue, his nervous
   Eye,
Mourning the Spirit grabbed inside out
   In the afreet of flesh,
Claiming each event had been a disease,
And to play its doctor part of the
   Etiology

Of life, one who followed a year
   behind you said
It was that home, that "far-off country
Neither of us wanted." Like him,

       You leave us stillborn poems:
       Their instar wings
       Murmuring near your ashes.

FAN

for Rick Rohdenberg

I used to believe I wouldn't live past 16:
That was Norm Siebern's number
And he seemed to me the epitome
    of minor, unspoken tragedy.
Stolid, St. Louis-German crewcut lefty with
Specs who hit a bunch of homers
And .290 for the Stengel Yankees, he blew
A Series game by dropping an easy fly
And was unloaded young on the Orioles, converted into
A 1st baseman, and hit nothing for a few dull summers
Before fading from the field—without a press conference or
    final trot around the bases.
I wanted to be Norm Siebern's son,
I wanted a father who could chaw Red Chief
And know how to shut up and leave things alone
While Baltimore won a pennant without him.
I knew Norm would never reach the Sunday averages or 20
Homers again, yet whenever I was at the stadium
I would scream for him to be put in:
He still had that amber Yankee lefty
Stroke—though too slow now—
And had resigned himself to pinch-hitting with the calm
Of a Chūshingura rōnin.
(Once he even led the league in walks, i.e.
    in patience.)
Whenever he hit into a double play
(He was almost as slow as Killebrew)
I would get so depressed that
It was impossible to do any more homework that night
For Mr. Axe, Miss Washing-machine, or
Miss Bitter . . . Norm,
                Dad,
One afternoon we were playing a doubleheader against the Angels
I had a box with that brat Jay DeMarco and his father

Right behind 3rd base and kept screaming at Bauer
        to put you in.
He didn't, but in the middle of the 5th of the last game
You stared at me like an ostrich over top of the dugout,
Disappeared, then rose like Boog Powell or Hondo Howard
(I never dreamed you were so big!) and gave me
Silently, nodding
One of your own
Cracked bats, your name
Looped into the fat, ash barrel.
That shut me up for a while . . . Norm,
Do you remember? No washed-up .240 choke was ever rooted for
As you were by me—none of my friends
Could fathom it, but
Can you root
        for me now?
I'm writing this so I won't kill myself
I never thought I'd get past your number
But here I am still fanning, still
Fouling everything off. I think it's because I never
Had a good year with the Yankees
And therefore can't go out with grace,
Personal honor, or be stoical about the stats. . . .
Is that it?
O, Silent batsman kneeling lonely
In the dark outfields of obscurity!
All night I've been shaking the old bat
Searching its fault for your secret.

The disciples gather in the great port
But sidestep the marketplaces.
They weep They either wish an end
To the Great Law of Change, or that a miraculous
Change would happen: the Master
Coming back or, denied that,

They want to see grieving trees turn white,
Puppies, calves born two-headed,
The wave tips in the harbor curve
                    into glimmering tongues
The sobbing fish can speak through.
But nothing changes.
                    Shikō
Gathers the last scroll of poems
tabi ni yande
One of them unfinished.
                    The ink slab
Seems to glow beside
The mat on which the Master died,
And one can almost hear the quick
Scraping of his stone across it. A stream

Of moonlight pierces the thatch
And we find, under his
Shit-soiled clothes
A clumsy beetle
Lifting, stumbling

CATCHING THE BUS ON A WINTER EVENING

Hot black water
from the laundromat drain

Burst the cells of what
grass in its path,

Shoved through snow
to the pavement where (steam) it drifted

from the cracks: rose, opened
from the blurred salt seed. Hung screens

on the air where headlights flung
ghosts that shook my observing brain

When the true bodies, talking, came undetained
through the crowding mist. I stand there numb,

I wait for the bus, schooled to see
Heaps of souls unfurling in steam,

Or warm libations of ox blood
gleaming in the gutter,

To envision the fog as Illusion
Baiting us from

Buddha-teeming absolutes.
I stand in a dream, in the tea-like taste of these

Bought thoughts. "Mind," I whisper,
"You are smoke once more."

I sit near the back, next to a boy
reeking of reefer and Nyquil,

Hugging his loud
radio to fill

Some vital, endless need.
Heavy with oil, with the refined

Remains of animal, tree
The heated air rises: noxious,

Sweet, condensing on my cold
window and lips.

TWO POEMS FOR GREGORY CRANE

June 1991

no longer hallucinatore
I began to look paintings again
and wondered suddenly where they came from

& hoped ô that beneath it all
some mebbed hellix bestreets it all?

in the landscape: at least 5 paths
each to a different center
things lit from afar
but far-off themselves, in a polished light
that didn't flash but persisted

a blade field between us
trilting

Red Thread

figurations forever transformacea
tangled trampled
but organ lace forming w between
in the flattened loops,
above 9 white tulips

splayed in a blooding
fan-fayre

> *If a bird were to paint would it not be by letting fall its feathers,*
> *a snake by casting off its scales, a tree by letting fall its leaves?*
> —Chaka Khan

I

The walls of the room have vanished.
There is just the one glandular light
Swinging, and the mattress
With its skin flayed off.

II

Dyer crawls out of the black bathroom.
His shadow—a spilling over of that blackness—
On the planked floor has two curved tusks.

III

A man sleeps under a parasol.
His noon-raw back is like a bleached elephant trunk.
Two grey cloth mares
Approach him flank by flank
Out of the blue beach.

Their miserable long-faced riders are so tall
Their boot tips almost
Clip the sand.
But the paper-thin horsebacks
Adze along their bloody groins.
If I focus there with this oil crayon
I find new lips instead of testicle.

IV

Your shadow is in front of you.
Like most others it is black
Except that at the collarbone
Warms one sun
A bile medallion
A hormonal zone burning.

Or perhaps something you ate yesterday:
The plaster off the wall joists
The hoof tracks on the shore
The jaundiced lightbulb in the soot flat
That you had been watching for so long
Like a bullfrog fixing
Frame by frame on a cricket.

V

Did we see you put it there
To train and observe us, to
Pin us outside your open cells?
Oh, how our overcoats fooled us!

1982

I

My professor often lost control of the wheel and I would take over
until he returned to his senses. He still had the pedals though, and we
went flowing out across refineries, marshes, loading docks, wharves in
fog that only a single tall foundry flame affixed in the sky like a bright
magnet.

As we went from reception to reception, he was so drunk that he
always forgot that my door was locked and I had to squeeze into the
sportster's red seat by approaching it from the white slope of its rear and
hopping in; later, when he put the top down, I was able to unlock it
myself by just leaning over, but why throw out a perfectly good
routine? At Teaneck, I stood up grasping the top of the windshield in
my right hand when he floored the gas pedal. As I guided the wheel
with my left hand, he—leaning out over his unlocked door—put his face
close to the front left tire and waved his arms around to grab bouquets
of exhaust as they burst by, dreaming they were pretty faces in Shinjuku.
Jack Daniels threading the air around us, he settled back into his seat and
began playing with the turn signals, grinning about how he sometimes
just wanted to reach out and kiss a whole armful of Tokyo girls as they
trot by, elbows linked in the summertime. I entrusted him with the
wheel and he yelled I could sit down now but I stretched up instead,
holding on to the windshield as all the trees planted by famous Ameri-
cans went by. As I waved to them, the clouds seemed to melt into
luscious bands of confetti.

II

I returned along a parallel street that licked itself between the two halves
of the army base. There, in the amber light of the evening Uigurs and
Gitanes sold their wares, placed out on surplus blankets. Not only along
the barb-crowned walls, but right out on the cobblestone thoroughfare
as well. Thinking that if I continued in my present line of entertainment
I would become despicable, I lingered at the spread of one vendor
before continuing on to that night's engagement. I knew I should read
and think again and picked at his used books like musty pears. One title

caught my eye: *The Japanese Sonnet*. I grinned cynically, thinking that it was another superficial and vanity-published study by some White Demon/Asshole drawing flowery parallels between English and Oriental poesy.

I was curious, however, about what particular Japanese verse form he had discomfited with the comparison—*tanka*? *hokku*? I opened the slim volume and was surprised to find facing me, translated into English, a poem at least two or three times longer than any *waka*. I hastily counted the lines, thinking that it would turn out to be three linked five-line verses (not, strictly speaking, a form unto itself), but it turned out to be exactly fourteen lines and with a rhyme scheme that I hadn't known existed in Japanese poetry: *aaab cccb dddb* (the last two lines kept disappearing from my eyes as I looked at the page). I decided immediately that this pattern should govern my opening act at the banquet that night. While singing a song of such quatrains, I would throw the whipped cream during each of the first three lines and duck under the linen of a table during the fourth (*pie pie pie duck*)—all the while acting whimsical in the manner of the famed Parisian and Tyrolean comedy troupes of the Thirties and early Forties. I do not remember if I paid the mordant, probably illiterate vendor for the book—I don't even know if I left it there—but set off immediately for the grand pavilion, though only after making sure I had rubbed out with a wet fingernail any place where the brilliant author's name appeared on the langsamer vergehenden pages.

III

cheetah roaming stalking as seen through the horns of the wildebeests.
wildebeests changing directions as the cheetah overruns them, past
ranks.

communal hunts of lionesses (w/out lion), and of hyenas, howling like
the hag in a dickens novel.

diktis staking out a bit of grove with musk released when they get a twig
to pierce a gland beneath the eye, and by scent from a gland in their
hooves.

wraiths, columns of flies rising from the lake to mate a few hours in
the forest, encountered by flocks of birds who gorge themselves on
them. falling back into the water where they are swallowed down by
Moe Drabowsky.

The cheetah and the wildebeest. The wildebeest has no rescuers. Brought
down by a drove of harrying hyenas, each with a quick bite to its groin.
But lioness and cheetah clutch and hurtle the windpipe. The perpendicular
lines of approach of a lioness (success? 1 for 3 in groups, 1 for 5 alone; 30
mph. cheetah? up to 70 mph but only for short bursts, can be outlasted).
Hyenas much slower, but persistent.

for DL

"Lev tells me that if only the idea of sex with a man appealed to him, he'd marry me right away. (He assumes I want him!) But he felt it would only be a substitution—there'd always be a lack."

I was talking with Lee about the same thing on a clear November morning. It was Sunday and the first time I'd been to Brooklyn Heights. We kept going back and forth along the railing that faced the tall stegosaurus tail of Manhattan, engaged in the type of talk I may have had ten years before in prep school: self-images, fears of women, sexual anatomy, what our parents wanted us to do. It was rejuvenating—like the flat white and orange sides of the docked container ship below us, seagulls and all that; the mind cleared a little in the long-lost adolescent chatter, and we both knew we thought each other childish. A lot of people, in thick-knit sweaters and red or orange down vests left open like dirty life jackets, were out in the sunlight with their dogs.

One man, in ample yet taut flesh that looked as if it grew back each night after savage incidents, sat glowering on a cracked dark-green bench, his end of the leash wrapped tightly around a spiked wristband. He was sunning himself and watched both men and women go by like stripped sides of pork. Every time we passed him in our endless walk I instinctively drew closer to Lee, which was ridiculous considering his tiny frame and lack of fortitude. A boy in cashmere coat and cap rolled a bagel toward us.

Almost automatically I told Lee one of my favorite anecdotes. "Miles Davis once said, comma"—I made the curling gesture with a finger: "'Al Green is so sexy that, if he had one tit, I'd marry him right away.' But when I told this to Lev I took out the part about being sexy to make it apply to us—it's ideas and art Lev wants to share, or consume, so much: 'That reminds me of what Miles Davis once said about Al Green.' 'Oh yeah?' 'Do you know what he said?' 'Uhn, what'd he say?' 'If Al Green had just one tit I'd marry him right away.'"

Lee was listening, though something in his stare now seemed bored and critical. I continued:

"So Lev said, howling, 'Miles *would* say that!' but then he suddenly stopped, a bizarre grin twisting between his cheeks like a crumpled fender. Like he didn't know whether he would have said it himself."

But Lee also reacted with confusion, as if he were suspicious of why I was telling him this story about the anecdote. And as if I were too dense to be aware of the reason myself. Finally, he let his annoyance (I was always afraid of *annoying* Lee more than anything else) emerge the most as he snapped:

"Males have two mammaries just like women do. Haven't you noticed that about yourself? So I don't get it: Davis wanted him to undergo a mastectomy so he'd have only *one* breast? Besides, Al Green is a minister now."

"I know, but he still sings."

"Sings gospel."

"Boobs and breasts aren't the same thing."

Lee liked that, but only because he thought he'd made me show how much of a boor I was. He let out an ugly belch of a chuckle.

"Forget it," I said, growing lonelier with each word.

We left the waterfront and stumbling about inland pretended that the diners and cafés were all too crowded with families and groggy couples this Sunday brunch time, and said goodbye to each other. I knew that all the long subway ride and wait for the transfer back, I'd get angry thinking the whole afternoon, morning, and even the sympathy of last night had been a waste, I couldn't trust any of it, and that uptown I'd soon be relying again on my "crotch."

V

Going all over the shopping-center parking lot at night trying to find the exit, same place over and over. The normal exit blocked by ditch work on a buried pipe—a Mercury Cougar goes up over the works and out. But I can't dare the same; on the other hand, terrified of confronting an angry Alabaman deep in the cool of the night, I don't ask the cops in a cruiser either. But they might pick us up anyway—for driving around with a redhead in the lot long after the stores had closed.

I had come out after dinner to meet her. Had been feeling like I was suddenly becoming Alec Guiness with my wife and pigtailed, secret-spilling daughter at the table who this time, after telling me my wife goes to a doctor to ask what my diet should be, divulges that she receives most of her household money from him—all of this said excellently in the third person. "The said woman receives from her astute doctor more than her unsuspecting husband gives her."

In the old elevator (thickly polished brass mouldings along the quartz sides) I find my cock between the stand-up, clear vinyl leggings whose cold tops cut right below the bum of the spry older woman with whom I am sharing the elevation. I find myself totally at ease with her again and ask if I can join her in her apartment. She says, "Of course! As long as that crazy kid doesn't kill himself. . . ." Who's that, I wonder—a kept boy? He is wearing a yarmulke, is very small, young and brutally ordered around by her, and when he finally realizes he's an obstacle leaves the large, Goodwill Store-furnished living room—not, however, without cursing us with a heavy metal record on the hi-fi, which, while she lifts her cerulean, hip-hugging Roman jersey off, I reach over and Reject. Coming back to her, I realize how much her attraction depended on her remarkable eyes, mouth, and costume. Sitting now on the poly-urethaned floor, on her knees, she is like a four-foot-tall mound of tapioca with breasts I can hardly distinguish in the general downward mucking pile—it is as if she would lose all composure and go melting across the floor if I did not embrace her soon. Fucking an undefinable mass. The only part I can find a shape of is her vagina, beautifully defined beneath the oodling fluff, but this is only by inference from my penile sensations, which are becoming fewer and farther between as its nervous girth and the loss of muscle tone there make the area too large for me to fill. Soon I am poking at a cold void—the only sensation, very slight, being the stream of air that breaks and passes along my dick as a result of its moving forward and back in an empty medium that, none-theless, keeps shifting trying to better position itself.

•

"Screw! Fuck a duck!" she keeps screeching later as she mauls the cold, late-night chicken like a lioness. Long jeans, halter top, and sandals give her form again as she lays down on the yellow, biting couch. While she tells me about how she fled to Sweden to escape a crazed boyfriend she brings out and guts her "Three-Jewish-Grandmother kugel." When she can't find the spatula immediately she complains that all her roommate needs is a TV and cleaning lady. I joke that she seems to have forgotten that she's already played both sides of the samba-a-go-go record three times and that it sounds warped. "Screw! I hope you're satisfied now that I've served as your straightman or whatever," she retorts repeatedly as she shows me to the chipped, quadruple-locked door that I had started eyeing soon after we began competing to see who could yelp louder longer, both of us elbowing for room in her open eighth-story window, at the unexpected full moon above the dark-scaled Hudson and the sky-line of Hoboken, remarkably unlit across the river like a black and even bar graph.

GREEN

In rainy woods
I looked for a new word—
All the old ones
Had become numbers

At nightfall a huge crow
Yanked my tongue out.
From the inflammation grew this
One transparent snake-nerve,
Filament rippling with silver tox.

With its quick wag
I tapped the roots of thrilling trees
And measured the warmth that swirls
In the wet hoof-tracks of deer.

Excited, I stumbled out of the forest
Shielding five vials in each of which glowed
One emblem of my joys: "Here, at last, the proof
        for the hues of Rimbaud's
Blazing vowels!"

Under white sky, my father waited
At a fence along the pasture ridge,
Cleaning the tungsten storage box.
"He has to believe me now," I whispered.

Because of the sudden snow
The hill though small was hard to climb.
Cheeks aflame, my head burning
With Nature-love, I tightened the scarf
Around my neck and to the treeline

Gave one glance back
Only to find: Every thicket

Dumb with tinsel, that the soft snow
Held no beast's shadow, and that in this
Human winter

My tongue was once more slug and starless
In its charred cocoon.

사

1983

for BKS—더 착한작가

I

Winter kept us dull, covering
Tramps in forgetful snow—
Feeding a little life with new video.

Summer surprised us, showered from World Trade Centers
With economic indicators. Three stopped at a trash bin
And went on in sunlight (their only recovery),
And sat on warm pavement & yapped for an hour:
"Cleveland screwed me. . . ."
                              "Go tell it to the President. . . ."
                                          "I'm an American. . . ."
binbō

                    Ed Rowney, say something or
Resign!
              For you know the charts of stymied agencies
And scenarios where payloads beat down
And the populace has no shelter,
The dying no belief, and the soft bone
No hope of healing. Only
There is shadow under this rocket
(Come out from under that red rocket)
And I will show you something different

From your shadow at morning rising to meet you
Or your shadow at evening striding behind you;
I will show you, in Hiroshima
A shadow without
                    the human that cast it,
Radiation in a handful of flesh.

74

hi no oku ni
  botan kuzururu
sama wo mitsu

President Reagan, famous clairvoyant,
Has it up to his keister. Nonetheless voted
Best man in America
With a wicked pack of cards. Here, said he,
Is a Commie airstrip in Grenada
(Those are Russians beneath the trees, look!)
Here is Nicaragua, a country of Reds
Here an SS-20 with three warheads,
And this slide, which I've just declassified,
Is what the Soviet hides in Cam Ranh Bay,
Which I am learning to say. I do not want
A test ban. Fear death by peace.
I see lots of Marines floating round on starships. . . .
Thanks and God Bless. Oh, if you see
Dear Clark or Adelman, tell them
I bring the horrorscope myself;
One must be so careful these days.

Under the rust of a winter dusk,
A crowd flowed over Williamsburg Bridge.
Sighs, long and tenuous, were exhaled
And all looked for supper beneath their feet.
Flowed up Sixth Ave to 32nd Street
To where Penn Station drags out the hours
With a fat cop on the final stroke of three.
There I saw one I knew and stopped him, crying:
"You who were with me in the gunships at My Lai!
The corpses we planted in the paddy,
Have they begun to sprout? Will they bloom this year?
You!" Hypocrite défenseur —
                    mon semblable, mon frère

II. A Game of Missile Command

> The Air Force believes these kids will be outstanding pilots,
> should they fly our jets. . . . Watch a 12-year-old take
> evasive action and score multiple hits while playing "Space
> Invaders" and you will appreciate the skills of tomorrow's
> pilot. . . . Right now you're being prepared for tomorrow in
> many ways—and in ways that many of us who are older
> cannot fully comprehend.
>
> —President Reagan,
> to high school students at the Epcot Center

             Beam him up at eight
And if it rains
We'll play a round of "Missile Command"
Pushing blue buttons and scanning for
God's knock upon the door.

A cockroach crept slowly through the detritus,
Dragging its feelers along the bank
While I was decaying in a charred hotel
On a rainy evening behind the stadium,
Musing upon my roommate, such a wreck:
Hurt flab naked on a low damp cot
And needles cast in a rusted-out tin,
While through my back I sometimes hear
les voix des enfants coréens
                brûlant à Nagasaki!

Shit shit shit
Fuh fuh fuh fuh
So rudely forced

        Unreal City,
Under a white dome on a winter noon,
The Secretary of Defense, slate-eyed

With a satchel full of toys
(DHL Northrop, diskettes out of sight)
Asked Congress to invest in Hell,
Followed by a weekend inside the Liberty Bell.

O City City, I can sometimes hear
Outside a bar on the Lower West Side
The whining of boys
And a clatter and chatter from within,
Where tight jeans lunge at noon
And posters of movie stars hold
Absolute splendor of
U.S. rawhide and gold.

    Sweatshops & factories:
"Rockefeller bore me. Toyota
Undid me. To Tokyo I raised my pleas
Supine on the floor of an extinct economy."

    Boom lacka lackalacka

    "During the recession,
I felt no remorse.
        I stayed the new course!
They made no comment.
What can they prevent?"

    Boom lacka

To Grand Concourse then I came

    Burning burning burning
O Lord Thou pluckest the South Bronx
O Lord Thou pluckest Overtown
O Lord Thou

burning

III. August, 1945

The Japanese colonial government forced over two million Koreans to work in military construction camps, brothels, mines, and factories. Nearly 20,000 died in the two atomic bombings.

Yi from Pusan,
Among so many dead,
Gained no independence.
                    Though the liberator he hadn't seen
Also plucked Mitsubishi clean.

As he burned and fell apart, he passed
The rages of his age and youth,
Not thinking such hell would last.

                    Oh Yankee or Red,
You who watch the radar
                    and can't hear the dead,
Remember Yi—who was once
Handsome and good as you.

IV. What the Pyŏrak Said

What is that island over the seas
Cracks and reforms and bursts in the violet air
Perforated atolls
Enewetok   Moruroa
Christmas Island
Unreal

A woman drew her hair out tight,
Then let it fan across the keloids on her back.
She runs a shop near Taegu now
In southeast Korea, near a village where four hundred
Forsaken live like lepers. If you speak to her
In Korean, she doesn't remember. It's only
The colonial tongue—ilbon mal—that can salve open
The hell in her brain. "I would kill myself now," she says
じさつするほうが 하지만
"But I must take care of my grandson. . . ."
(She points off-screen at a deformed young man.)
In the violet light
The newborn with bent faces
Whistled and beat their wings
And crawled head downward down blackened walls.
Scorched temples tolled antiquated bells
While voices faded in contaminated wells.
Nuked bones can harm no one.

DA
      Im: After the bombing, the few doctors
Would only treat Japanese. So I
Went off with the rest
To die in the hills.
DA
      Yi: What have we given, my friend?
Blood shaking the world

That an age of programs can never retract.
By this we have resisted,
Which cannot be found in Monbushō books
Or diplomatic calls for peace.
DA
        Chŏng: The kayagŭm responded gaily
To the hand expert with pluck and bend.
The drum was calm, your heart would have responded
Gaily, if amnesiac,
           beating obedient
To the songs of our land.

      I crouched in a foxhole in Nevada
With the fallout close upon me.
Shall I at least set my limbs in order?
Shinbashi is falling down falling down
O Cruise cruise!
MX, Pershing, Trident
Le roi d'Amérique à la tour abolie
SS-20, -13, -4. . . .
Bin gar keine Russin, stamm' aus Litauen
Laser beams, particle beams, enhanced
Radiation: Teller's mad againe!
These sandbags deter against my ruin
Why then I'll BEAT you
Kono yo mo nagori
  yo mo nagori
Shini ni yuki mi wo
             tatōreba

Dave became Dr. Koski!
I, an accountant

Sub figures in my chest
Where, gassed-up rumor
My heart had been

Slung too early
From the carrier deck,
Struck wing

Trailing cracks
Through the hard night till explosion
Over Laos. Dave,
I recall in Da Nang, 2 weeks

Before discharge home
You started crawling to the john,
Took shits with a ripe

Grenade in each fist, cleaned
Carbine across your lap;
You were not going to let no idiot

Raid of slant-eyes with Chink
AK burn your ass so close to
Flying back to Pawtucket, back to

Good booze and real white ass.
As the last dawn neared
You even smashed the radio, its rock & roll,

Became quiet as a monk
Of your departure. When the chopper came
You said "You know, next to an

American, I'll always want
A Koo-rean fighting beside me."
Meaning the hardass ROK platoons

Pushing up with us
That August, but hell, I was raised
In Chicago, on Clark

With Mexican, Bloods, and slab-faced
Poles like you! Didn't give my address,
Fearing you or a buddy

Might rape my wife
In some wrecked dream of revenge.
Your bird

Went up at noon,
Slicing dust in my face,
Bending me back like bamboo

Or ripe rows of rice shoot.
Eight more months I stayed on,
Cutting down gook like crazy, then

Came home to school, hid
Between the pages, scanned
The equations, indices, charts

And followed along the mute
Graphs right up into
The blank spaces.

fractured unspeakens
nothing for the TeleDrive
Subjonctif: flogged schwarzkoffin, sadie &
boy gorge (c.i.f. bechtel, diskettes out of sight)
with guard flank dripping uranium
marinade. what's that, some type of
Memory or something?

Underdone. Sous & fait.
Il souhaite. Skin legs and all

1991

MAL

"대한 독립 만세!" "우리 나라 만세!"
목청이 터져라고 불렀읍니다.
손에 손에, 태극기를 들고, 우 관순은 땅은
사람들과 같이, 소리 높이 만세를 불렀읍니다.

Fig. 5 : les symboles de l'abondance et de la vitesse des cultures.

어머니에게 드리는 말

기미년 3월 1일. 외당순 양성회 신생님
표에 33인이서명한 독립 선언서가. 탁생내
표에 의하여, 파고다 공원에서 인쇄됨
으로써, 노도같은 만세의 물결은 터젓
읍니다. 저마풍들에게는, 3·1운동의 역사
저 배경과 진상을 설명해 주고, "만세"
의 뜻을 완도들 함께 순시다. 그리고,
"독립 선언서"란 무엇인가를 가르쳐 주
십시다.

충 길 앞에, 번 주먹으로는, 싸울 수 없
읍니다. 유 권순 누나는, 끝내, 일본 헌병
들에게 잡혀서 죽었읍니다.

동생들이 밤 하늘을 쳐다 봅니다.

"누나 별은, 어느 별?"

"누나 별이 타네, 훨훨 타네/"

누나를 그리워하는 동생의 작은 주먹
이, 눈물을 씻습니다. 별들이 반짝입니다.

Fig. 2 : le mythe du retour.

말

I toss apple peel from the clinic's window into the alley. I thought the food stall below had closed, but suddenly I hear an older woman's voice explode in a long, screeching tirade. After turning out the light, I go back to the window and see an ajuma in drab sweater, functional perm, and loose, ankle-length smock rush away around the corner with a newspaper-tented dinner tray—probably for tired hostesses at a nearby bar. Her rant against whoever the son-of-a-bitch threw trash down in front of her restaurant: it delighted me! I felt so close to her, I took it as proof that, at least momentarily, I was part of the local scene, though unseen receded into the darkness of my room, unable to push back yet.

10/19/85

Dear Lewis,

I'm at *another* aunt's this weekend. I'm in the anbang (the living room of a Korean house), sitting on the floor watching boring TV, and very comfortable. In one corner a cousin is knitting a sweater, in the other her 9-month-old son has finally run out of magazine-tearing, dish-biting, food-hurling energy and is asleep between tiny quilts on a pillow. A few feet away from him, the tall "mixed-blood" maid from the countryside in brown corduroy slacks and red sweater is also knitting while sitting cross-legged on the floor, her strong back and shoulders remarkably straight against the mirror on the wall behind her. Now my aunt, after placing her newly permed head on an upright roll of toilet paper as a headrest, is also falling asleep, knees bent, billowing bottom facing her grandson. I planned to write you a long letter straight through the afternoon, but I think I'll also take a nap now, guarded from bad spirits by the click and draw of the two young women's smooth needles.

2/16/86

A beautiful *Coca-Cola* truck was parked outside the breakfast shop. Long chrome klaxon on a white cab roof, like the enameled lids of a tin tea-sampler set. Wherever I've gone, my love, Coke was there to tempt me: in the dusty People's Park in Shanghai, a Ming wall near Mongolia, every teahouse and subway station in Seoul and Tokyo. And rather than enter new physiological states in foreign places, I often surrendered, reticular mumbling in confusion, and became instead a Cola-head, zappity on the caff, then veering from the sucrose feed, thirsting for the sleep arms of a mama-box.

6/86

SEOUL: WINTER, 1986

There was a question in a popular book.
On the cover was a painting—part of
The old effort: Horses, riverbank, willow tree,
Escort, on the front 文化 shelf.
Across the aisle: Heat Transfer, COBOL, thick
Con books for the English-as-a-Foreign-Language exam
For those who would study in the realm

I left for the land my parents escaped
Here: I browse between shelves for identity
And shelves for progress, wealth
   and can't
Rage in opposition
I had left both sides
               The question was on the page
I opened to.
I skipped the chapter's title.
The author's name was writ in Chinese
His family name was Kim!
               It asked, When
Is a woman most beautiful: While sewing
While reading or
Weeping?
        I thought of my swirling
Mistress and whispered,
While leaving almost
Quiet enough for
No one to hear.

ON THE ROAD TO THE BLUE HOUSE WITH CBS NEWS IN SEOUL

I ebb I lie in my strait. the
jesus trees waving liek fire hydren
over the roofs. if it were seoul but
it cant be. if it were '87 summer but then
it cant be can it. June. if nevr sensed
time moves forwrd then it might move
back right   I
durn I strain in my
lit the whole world carmine neon
jassus trees burning bending stranding   To
Yoido then we came, burning   plazas
Whirring two million voters won by
tins of cooking oil cheering
in front of a fusillade of foreign
camera   Pointing like us   just
the too of us

IN AN ALLEY

No stars in the blank serenade of this night
Neon showers up from downtown, out-town
And at the noodle wagon as the harsh lover who always
Lies to make me smile pours more soju out
I stare at my light hands holding up the short glass
As if they were about to fade. And all this

Is suddenly not what I need anymore.
The soft, huddled veins are so calm right now
I wish someone would drape them in a cool
Crypt out of time. Do I know where one is?

•

Everywhere I lived I felt windswept and thin—
Bashō's bright heartless sun
Dissolving into ember dark edges of my dream

Like film slowly combusting,
Looped tiaras of rejected vision
Unraveling at dusk in a ditch.

At my age, forlorn Sowŏl
Cried beneath a black hinge
Of winter geese that,
Though he was at the center of many crossroads,

The paths branching and branching like
Spilled wine,
No road was his.

I have a path, I
Had a path
But no heart to follow it.

•

What have I done? At dusk near Chopyŏng,
Stung red kochu dripping pus,
I kneeled a long time before the burial mound
Of my mother's father and mother,
Weeding the clayey crown,
And waited for them to ask me that.
I don't know if they did or not, but I felt

Penitent down the dirt road to the village of my
Evil uncle. Sweet dung smell
Wept across the dry brown fields
By the road from my grandparents' graves.
All this, they said to my nape
Was ours once, stream and mountain.
Your fake uncle forged the will as we faded.
Should we take revenge?
                    Oh, I grinned
as I trudged the last hill,
That's why I see Uncle slip out the back door!

And when I sit inside on the twig-heated floor
his big wife and son keep nudging me:
U.S. must be good. Stay there!
We're poor. Hey, eat more of this.

                •

When I lift my bag, Uncle appears outside
Stabs one bill for carfare into my windbreaker.
Doesn't smile or wave.
                    A hen complains
I didn't bring enough cartons
of Winstons.
                    Cold ochre dust
Sweeps through the Kia cab
As we slam up the rutted road
To the new highway. The radio's loud:
Nasty skits about shamed lovers in Seoul, cheery
Laugh track. I scream like a drunk,

"How far to the bus station?"
Muddied hands cupped
Over my seeping root.

TREADWINDS

with collages by Lewis Klahr

I

Neighborhoods do
what the dead did—
welcome us without seeing us

after many years
I came back hungry
for that dumb giving

throwing longer shadows
lower along

            sidewalks & the jeweled
            wall above

      •

Halls, doorways: they do
what the gods did—
receive us without us

seeing them. When children
we entered and ran
thinking their mazes obvious

we return with less
than one life left

climbing a stairway
past the past

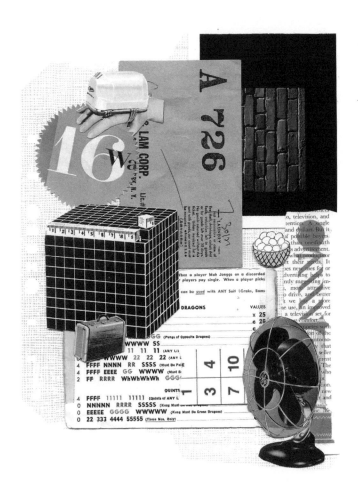

II

All day I sulked
like a fat trout circling
slowly above La Guardia.
Bridges passed over like a great beard.
I lay on a marble box beneath
The new memorial. Carved letters home
from soldiers slaved & brushed their teeth above,
in the August wind and glass light.

Nothing to touch, but this my shirt
medaled by the sun

Turned and whispered to stout white boats
churning their way
to the Jersey and Staten archipelago

dozed off stiff on a stone bench when
a trash gull burned its twisted
finger through my

flagging right shoulder. I am not a shank thing. I
thank my aery spirit for this. endless

mur mur in my spine

III

I returned to the hotel room. The notebook was open on
the round desk, and sunlight turned its pages; it fanned
like an ohia lehlua plant. I turned to my left and saw

mudlight
moontruck

bloodhope

bonegun

but found no tribe in all the
sheetskin and

stressrock

Hearts of Lettuce	.25	Fresh Lobster	1.00
Sliced Tomatoes	.20	Fresh Shrimp	.55
Cole Slaw	.15	Herring	.45
Potato	.15	Chicken	.60
Cucumber	.20	Lettuce and Tomatoes	.40

Combination .... .45

STEAKS AND CHOPS

Beef Steak	.75	Chopped Sirloin of Beef Steak	.65
Sirloin Minute Steak	.85	Schnitzel Naturel	.60
Bone Sirloin	1.00	Paprika Schnitzel with Noodles	.70
Broiled Tenderloin on Toast	1.00	Schnitzel a la Holstein	.75
Filet Mignon Broiled	1.10	Wiener Schnitzel	.65
Single Porterhouse Steak	1.25	Spring Lamb Chops (2)	.65
Sirloin for Two	1.90	Jersey Pork Chops (2)	.50

Filet Mig

Asparagus
String Beans
Spinach

German Fried
French Fried

Smothered Onions or Fried

COLD

Assorted Cold Cuts
Imported Cold Cuts
Westfalian Ham
Corned Brisket of Beef
Imported Cervelat

Ham	.15
Western	.25
Head Cheese	.25
Hamburger Steak	.30
Hot Prime Rib of Beef	.45
Imp. Swiss Cheese	.25
Sirloin Steak on Toast	

SANDWICH

Beef Tongue

Harzer H Kaese .25

RAREBITS

Welsh .50

CHEESE per P

Liederkranz
Roquefort
Limburger

DESSERTS

Puddings	.15	Ice Cream	.15
Pot of Tea		Milk	.10

IV

What are the sounds of spring—
Children outside in a playground?
Something else happened here.
Stale bread aching to fill a mouth,
Small coins shining on a sill as we
Tried to spend more than ourselves.

Wherever windlight
wells and walls
Not bed, not room or sky
Not in or out, but on, along
That was me from now on, I sighed:
Always people dwelling, birds singing
Beyond yet in my touchless spots

The pool is crazy once more!
Even large animals drink there

I eat timesalt.
Snails nod in the lagoon of my intestines

Drift on treadwinds,

Whims of a
wondered walker

MĀNOA RUN

If I stretch it out, turn and go

Up the hill, the circling road
Behind the widow's house

I will see an ocean sunset, flotillas

Of cirrus blazing in their chassis.
I will follow the curve, the lush bend up into the better

Neighborhood: silk dogs, children tumbling like deaf-mutes,

The crying paradisial flora
Shrubbed and rinsed and shaken clean.

A cold flame of wind will grab fallen, lung-sized

Kamani leaves and gust them into
A walking companion

Rushing and treading beside me, at shoulder height:

Its head's milled peat, belly, shins
Unceasingly thrashed and shat into each other,

As if this were no mere exercise

But a face of the hidden urge, whispered
Mind of things to pace and speak with us.

By this I will be made helpless, and jog on

Knowing like a scar, that I cannot remember, cannot
Say the spell exactly, or dare to embrace

The falling figure, weep and pray

For the burning prisoner kneeling into his
Dissolving shins. *Grandfather!* I may whisper, *Father!*

My father says all his life here. The flame withdraws,

The head keels, flops open like a gourd
Into a hopping gyre of mute leaves

On the black road, if I stop and turn around.

Notes

p. v, Dedication: The last two lines are from part 4 of T. S. Eliot's "East Coker."

p. 5: From Kim Sŭng-ok's short story "Mujin kihaeng" (Record of a Journey to Mujin). A translation by Kevin O'Rourke was published in *Korea Journal* 17.6 (June 1977).

p. 14: Dhāranī chart from the *Haein sammae ron* (Treatise on the Ocean Seal Samadhi) by Myŏnghyo. Dhāranī are brief texts that comprehensively encode the meanings of the Buddha's teachings. A translation of this Silla dynasty work (ca. 7th–8th century C.E.) is included in my master's thesis, "Against Counting Up Verses: Myŏnghyo's Polemic in the *Haein sammae ron*, a Silla Treatise based on the *Flower Garland Scripture*," University of California, Los Angeles, 1992.

pp. 20, 22, 27: Stills reproduced from Lee Young-il [Yi Yŏng-il], *The History of Korean Cinema/Han'guk yŏnghwa sa*, translated by Richard Lynn Greever (Seoul: Motion Picture Promotion Corp./Yŏnghwa Chinhŭng Kongsa, 1988). They are for the following movies, respectively: *Salsuch'a* (The Sprinkler Truck; dir. Pang Han-jun, 1935); *Sŏnghwangdang* (Village Shrine; dir. Pang Han-jun, 1939); *Nagŭne* (Wanderer; dir. Yi Kyu-hwan, 1937); *Kŭmbongŏ* (Goldfish; dir. Na Ŭn-gyu, 1927); *Mŏngt'ŏng'guri* (The Fool; dir. Yi P'il-u, 1926); *Tŭlchwi* (Field Rat; dir. Na Ŭn-gyu, 1927).

p. 31: "Feet that have kicked off their shoes stumble in mid-air." From the prose poem *Maech'un* by Yi Sang (b. 1910, d. 1937).

p. 45: A phonetic translation of the preceding dialogue, which is in "foreigner"'s Japanese.

p. 49: Charles Mingus, *Beneath the Underdog*, edited by Nel King (New York: Penguin, 1971).

p. 61: Epigraph from "What Is a Picture?," in *The Four Fundamental Concepts of Psycho-Analysis*, edited by Jacques-Alain Miller, translated by Alan Sheridan (1978; New York: W. W. Norton, 1981).

p. 73: *Sa*; common meanings include "four," "death," "history," "snake," "temple."

p. 75: "Hi no oku ni" is a haiku by Katō Shūson (b. 1905, d. 1993). Donald Keene's translation: "In the depths of the flames / I saw how a peony / Crumbles to pieces." In Donald Keene, ed., *Modern Japanese Literature* (New York: Grove, 1956).

p. 80: "Kono yo mo nagori" is spoken by the narrator of the *bunraku* puppet drama *Sonezaki shinjyu* (Love Suicides at Sonezaki) by Chikamatsu Monzaemon (b. 1653, d. 1725). Donald Keene's translation: "Farewell to the world, and to the night farewell. / We who walk the road to death, to what should we be likened?" In Donald Keene, ed., *Anthology of Japanese Literature from the Earliest Era to the Mid-Nineteenth Century* (New York: Grove, 1955).

p. 95: Super-8 film shot by the author in Seoul, 1987.

pp. 100, 102, 104–106: Collages by Lewis Klahr. Paper cut-outs on cardboard backgrounds, 1993. Courtesy of the artist. Originally part of the poetry video "Treadwinds" (dir. Lewis Klahr and Walter K. Lew, 1993), Poetry Spots series, WNET and WNYC-TV.

p. 111: Seoul, 1959.

Acknowledgments

Some of the pieces collected in this book previously appeared in the following publications: *Amerasia Journal*, *Arras*, *The Asian Pacific American Journal*, *Bamboo Ridge*, *Bold Words: A Century of Asian American Writing* (Rutgers University Press), *BOMB*, *Braided Lives: An Anthology of Multicultural American Writing* (Minnesota Humanities Commission), *Breaking Silence: An Anthology of Contemporary Asian American Poets* (Greenfield Review Press), *Bridge: Asian American Perspectives*, *Chain*, *Chicago Review*, *Xcp: Cross-Cultural Poetics*, Excerpts from: *ΔIKTH 딕 테 / 딕 티 DIKTE*, for *DICTEE* (1982) (Yeul Eum Sa), *Hanging Loose*, *Korea Magazine*, *The Literary World*, *New Worlds of Literature: Writings from America's Many Cultures* (W. W. Norton), *The Nuyorasian Anthology* (Asian American Writers Workshop), *Poet's Feet*, *Premonitions: The Kaya Anthology of New Asian North American Poetry* (Kaya Production), *Works in Progress*, *The World*.

Walter K. Lew's critical collage *Excerpts from: ⊿IKTH* 딕테/딕티 *DIKTE, for DICTEE* (1982) was published in 1992, and he is currently preparing a translation with commentary of the selected works of Yi Sang. Lew has edited and written essays for *Crazy Melon and Chinese Apple: The Poems of Frances Chung* (Wesleyan, 2000), the poetry anthology *Premonitions* (1995), and *Muae I* (1995), and co-edited *Kŏri: The Beacon Anthology of Korean American Fiction* with Heinz Insu Fenkl (2001). Lew's work as a documentary and television news producer has been broadcast on numerous networks, and he has collaborated with filmmaker Lewis Klahr to create multimedia pieces performed at international film festivals in the United States and South Korea. The recipient of grants from the National Endowment for the Arts, New York State Council on the Arts, Association for Asian Studies, and Korean Culture and Arts Foundation, Lew has taught at Brown, Cornell, and the University of California, Los Angeles.

Library of Congress Cataloging-in-Publication Data
Lew, Walter K.
    Treadwinds : poems and intermedia texts / Walter K. Lew.
    p. cm.
    ISBN 0-8195-6509-1 (alk. paper) —
    ISBN 0-8195-6510-5 (pbk. : alk. paper)
    1. Korean Americans—Poetry.
    2. Korea—Poetry. I. Title.
    PS3612.E844 T74 2002
    811'.6—dc21   2002016760